THE PERFECT LIFE?

SIN, THE SOUL, AND KINGDOM LIVING

GRAND RAPIDS, MICHIGAN 49530 USA

Youth Specialties

www.youthspecialties.com

The Perfect Life? Leader's Guide
by Rick Bundschuh
Copyright © 2005 by Youth Specialties
Youth Specialties Books, 300 South Pierce Street, El Cajon, CA 92020, are published by Zondervan, 5300 Patterson Avenue SE, Grand Rapids, MI 49530

Library of Congress Cataloging-in-Publication Data

Bundschuh, Rick, 1951-
  The perfect life? leader's guide : sin, the soul, and kingdom living / by Rick Bundschuh.
    p. cm.
  ISBN-10: 0-310-25839-1 (pbk.)
  ISBN-13: 978-0-310-25839-1 (pbk.)
  1. Church work with teenagers. 2. Teenagers--Religious life. I. Title.
BV4447.B776 2005
268'.433--dc22

2005011798

Unless otherwise indicated, all Scripture quotations are taken from the Holy Bible: New International Version (North American Edition). Copyright © 1973, 1978, 1984 by International Bible Society. Used by permission of Zondervan Publishing House.

Some of the anecdotal illustrations in this book are true to life and are included with the permission of the persons involved. All other illustrations are composites of real situations, and any resemblance to people living or dead is coincidental.

All rights reserved. No part of this publication may be reproduced, stored in a retrieval system, or transmitted in any form or by any means—electronic, mechanical, photocopy, recording, or any other—(except for brief quotations in printed reviews), without the prior permission of the publisher.

Web site addresses listed in this book were current at the time of publication. Please contact Youth Specialties via e-mail (YS@YouthSpecialties.com) to report URLs that are no longer operational and replacement URLs if available.

Editorial direction and editing by Dave Urbanski
Proofread by Laura Gross and Heather Haggerty
Cover and interior design by proxy

Printed in the United States of America

06 07 08 09 / 10 9 8 7 6 5 4 3 2

07	The Perfect Guy	1
21	Transformation	2
33	The Good Pens	3
49	Christen Cross Journey Story	4
61	The Sin Vibe	5

HIGHWAY VISUAL CURRICULUM

Volume Five

THE PERFECT LIFE?

Introduction

Welcome to Youth Specialties and Highway Video.

Unlike many teaching tools, Highway Video does not presume to tell you what message to communicate to your flock. Instead, it is designed to be a flexible tool you can use to work with whatever message, purpose, and age level you have. Everything from announcements and teaching moments to benedictions, this material can be used with every age level—from middle school kids on up—and for just about any group size and church style.

But we don't want to leave you hanging.

In this booklet we've provided ideas for a variety of ways you can use each film clip. We've also included a lesson plan or two for you to check out and plug in wherever you feel it's appropriate. The lessons written for middle school students are short and action-filled. Those written for high school groups are longer with less action but more abstract thinking.

Our lesson plans even have downloadable, reproducible talksheets and other activity resources. You can download them for free off this Web site:
www.YouthSpecialties.com/store/downloads
code word: highway 5

To indicate each possible option for using a particular film clip, we've created a **Signpost icon**. This symbol designates a new path of teaching or communication for the video segment. With just a glance you'll be able to access a wide expanse of alternatives for using each video clip with your group.

Please feel free to manipulate the video in whatever way works best for your purposes.

For example, you may only want to show a portion of the video. Or you may decide that your group should view the clip more than once, maybe showing it to them a second time after you've explored the subject—just as a reminder.

You may download the video into your computer video editing program and clip the time, add a trailer, insert some Scripture, or use whatever devices you have at your disposal that will help you communicate the point of your lesson or message.

Look for **Production Notes** and its icon to get behind-the-scenes comments from the producers.

For a couple of the Signposts we have gone ahead and mapped out lesson plans for youth groups that support a particular teaching idea inspired from the film clip. Remember, the talksheet resources for these lessons are integrated in these texts, but they can be downloaded and customized for your use—free of charge—at
**www.YouthSpecialties.com/store/downloads
code word: highway 5**

The Perfect Guy 1

Alternate Routes

 General Church Use

This nutty video clip might just be the ticket as a comic prelude to an announcement encouraging people to sign up for a marriage enrichment seminar—or better yet, for singles—or as a discussion starter in a home Bible study or something similar. Float this one around; you might be surprised who wants to use it.

 Small Group

Focus: Our unrealistic expectations can result in disappointment with God

Biblical basis: Matthew 19:16-22, 22:36-40; Luke 7:20, 23:8-11; John 6:59-61

Stuff you need: paper, pencils, *The Perfect Guy* video clip

Getting Started

Use *The Perfect Guy* video clip as a discussion starter. Introduce it by saying something like:

> **Let's start by taking a look at a clever commentary on relationships. As you watch this, see if you relate more to the girl who's narrating or to the guys in this video clip called—what else?—*The Perfect Guy*.**

The Perfect Guy Video Clip

Show the clip to your group, and then follow up by asking what message they got from the video. Drop a few questions like these into the mix:

- Do you think the problem rested with the girl's unrealistic expectations or with the knuckleheads she was dating?

- What happens if our expectations of another person aren't realistic?

- Have you ever felt someone expected more out of you than you could possibly give?

- All relationships, not just romantic ones, take work and compromise. What do the filmmakers suggest by the end of the clip?

Bible Study

Ask—Do you think people were disappointed with Jesus? Why or why not? Let's read some of these passages and see.

- Luke 7:20 (John the Baptist questions if Jesus is the real deal)

- Luke 23:8-11 (Herod gets no satisfaction)

- John 6:59-61 (Dissatisfied disciples)

- Matthew 19:16-22 (Rich Man Blues)

Now ask—

- In what way did Jesus disappoint the people in these passages?

- What were people expecting, and what did they get?

- Do you know anyone who believes God either didn't meet their expectations or let them down? Explain why they feel this way.

- Do you feel any pity or empathy for people who don't like God's answers (or lack of them) and ultimately give up on God?

- What happens when you're saddled with expectations you can't meet?

- What happens to relationships riddled with unfair expectations?

- What should you do if you are experiencing a "perfect guy" (or girl!) moment?

Wrap Up

Pass out paper and pencils. Ask for volunteers to finish this sentence: "I will probably disappoint people if they expect me to _____." Ask a few people to share their answers, and then thank them for their honesty.

Read aloud Matthew 22:36-40: "'Teacher, which is the greatest commandment in the Law?' Jesus replied: 'Love the Lord your God with all your heart and with all your soul and with all your mind.' This is the first and greatest commandment. And the second is like it: 'Love your neighbor as yourself.' All the Law and the Prophets hang on these two commandments."

Remind the group that our expectations of others ought to reflect this kind of generosity of spirit.

Close in prayer.

Middle School

Focus: God uses less-than-perfect people—people we'd never expect

Biblical basis: Joshua 2:1-21; Matthew 8:5-13, 9:9-10; Luke 5:1-11, 21:1-4; 1 Corinthians 1:26-29

Stuff you need: Barbie and Ken dolls, 11x17 sheets of paper, pencils, markers, *The Perfect Guy* video clip

Getting Started

Bring a Barbie doll and a Ken doll to the meeting. Hold them up and share this little bit of trivia:

> Most little kids grow up thinking that these two dolls represent the ideal man and woman. Well, do I have some interesting news for you! If Barbie were a real woman, she'd be seven-feet tall. Her bust would measure between 38 and 40 inches, her waist between 18 and 24 inches, and her hips between 33 and 35 inches. Barbie's weight would be 110 pounds. If she were a real woman, Barbie would have to walk on all fours due to her proportions.
>
> If Ken were a real man, he'd be seven-feet, eight-inches tall. His chest would be about seven inches larger than the average man's, and his neck would be about eight inches larger. Needless to say, this ideal couple isn't so ideal in real life.

Transition to *The Perfect Guy* video clip by saying something like this:

> **We live in a world where the need to be "perfect" is portrayed by every magazine and movie. Many people invest tons of money to look perfect through plastic surgery; and many people are secretly**

```
The Perfect Guy
vol  chp  pg
05:  01:  11
```

fearful that unless they appear cool, wealthy, and physically attractive, they're doomed. Perfection is the theme of this little film satire. Let's check it out.

▶ *The Perfect Guy* Video Clip

Show the clip and then invite comments after the film ends. Now transition to the Bible study by saying something like this:

> It's very interesting whom God chose as his friends and followers—those who ultimately carried his message to the world. Let's take a look at what makes someone really important and attractive in this world.

Bible Study

Divide your students into groups of two or three and assign each group one of the following passages:

- Joshua 2:1-21 (A soiled dove does right by God)
- Matthew 8:5-13 (The enemy soldier who's the example of faith)
- Matthew 9:9-10 (A crook becomes an apostle and a writer of a gospel)
- Luke 5:1-11 (The fishermen who became apostles)
- Luke 21:1-4 (The widow who Jesus said was the best example of a giver)

Pass out paper (11x17 is the best size), pencils, and markers. Tell your students they are now paparazzi photographers and reporters for a tabloid-style gossip publication (akin to *The*

National Enquirer or *Star*). Each group should read their assigned passage about someone God used to impact others and then dream up a cover story—complete with pictures—that emphasizes what an odd selection that person was for the job. (For instance, a headline like, "THIS PERSON IS SUPPOSED TO BE A GOOD EXAMPLE?") Naturally the idea is to make the story sing with exaggeration while still maintaining an element of truth. Tell the groups that drawing "photos" to support their headlines will help.

After your students have read their passages and worked up their cover stories, ask them to share them with everyone.

Now share 1 Corinthians 1:26-29 with your students: "But God chose the foolish things of the world to shame the wise; God chose the weak things of the world to shame the strong" (v. 27). Ask—

- What does this tell you about the kinds of people God uses to do great things for him?

- What hope does that give to people who are less than perfect?

- Why do you think God typically uses people who aren't big stars—even when he could get more "publicity" with bigger names?

Wrap Up

Pass out pencils and paper to your group. Ask your students to consider what God has done for those who are less than perfect and then fill in the following statement: "I know that even though I'm not perfect, _____." Close in prayer.

High School

Focus: We often have unrealistic expectations of God and of others

Biblical basis: Matthew 19:16-22; Luke 7:20, 23:8-11; John 6:55-66; 1 Corinthians 13; 1 Peter 4:19

Stuff you need: pencils, paper, *The Perfect Guy* video clip, copies of What Guys Are Like (page17) and What Girls Are Like (page18) Talksheets (a free download is available at www.YouthSpecialties.com/store/downloads code: highway 5)

Getting Started

Idea #1: Divide your group into guys and girls. Ask each group to come up with a top-10 list of things that make the perfect guy or girl. (Naturally, guys should come up with the list for the perfect girl, and girls will make a list for the perfect guy.) Have your groups come back together and share their lists with everyone. (Be prepared for daggers and groans.)

Transition to *The Perfect Guy* video clip by saying something like this:

> You obviously have some high expectations—so let's watch a video where a young woman also has some expectations of her "perfect guy."

Play the clip, and then roll into the Bible study by commenting:

> It's normal to have unrealistic expectations at times. Let's take a few minutes and see if we can clarify what men and women should reasonably expect from each other. And to get that picture in our minds, we need to start with God's Word.

Idea #2: Ask your students to share about someone else's annoying habit (chewing fingernails, talking on the cell phone all the time, and so on)—make sure they don't use names! Then ask if they have any habits that others might find annoying.

Transition to *The Perfect Guy* video clip by saying something like this:

> **We all have little quirks that can annoy others after a while. Most of our friends learn to put up with it. But for some, perfection is the only answer. Let's check out a loony video clip that comments on the expectations some people have of others.**

Show *The Perfect Guy* video clip and invite comments after the clip.

Bible Study

Idea #1: If they aren't already divided this way, ask your students to move into two groups—guys only and girls only. Give the girls copies of the What Guys Are Like (page 17) Talksheet, and give the guys copies of the What Girls Are Like (page 18) Talksheet.

(You can download both of these sheets for free at www.YouthSpecialties.com/store/downloads code: highway 5.)

All groups will need pens or pencils as well.

Ask your students to fill out the worksheets as honestly as possible and keep them anonymous. After a few minutes, collect the worksheets. Have a staff person add up the scores and bring back a final tally.

While this is going on, ask your students to turn to 1 Corinthians 13 and carefully go over this great chapter on love. (It'd be a good idea to use a few different versions for the sake of comparison.) Discuss the attributes of this godly love and see if your kids agree that it should be the standard of love—including for those with whom we desire a romantic relationship.

When the worksheets have been tallied, read the results. (Again be prepared for howls of disagreement!) Then use the questions on the worksheets as points of discussion relating back to the definition of love for another person.

Idea #2: Discuss with your group the idea that even Jesus didn't live up to others' expectations. Ask your students to break into pairs, give each group one of the following passages to explore, and then pass out paper and pencils. The students should answer the following questions about their assigned Scripture: In what way did Jesus disappoint the people in your passage? and What were people expecting, and what did they get?

- Luke 7:20 (John the Baptist questions if Jesus is the real deal)
- Luke 23:8-11 (Herod gets no satisfaction)
- John 6:55-66 (Dissatisfied disciples)
- Matthew 19:16-22 (Rich Man Blues)

Have your students report back what they discover. Then ask—

- Do you know people who feel as though God didn't meet their expectations or he let them down? Explain why they might feel this way.

- How would you assure them that God can be counted on or explain that their expectations are misplaced?

Wrap Up

Idea #1: Use this idea if you've been working on the guy and girl lesson. Pass out new sheets of paper. Ask your students to consider all the things that have been discussed about guy-girl relationships, and then write down one thing they might do or say differently based on what they've heard today. Close in prayer.

Idea #2: Ask your students to read 1 Peter 4:19 and come up with one word that defines God in a way that will satisfy those who feel he hasn't lived up to their expectations. Share that word and why it was selected. Close in prayer.

What Guys Are Like Talksheet

Please answer the following questions as honestly as you can. When you circle your answers, don't think about a specific guy or only guys who call themselves Christians—think about guys in general.

1. Most guys have no clue about how to act in front of girls they like.

    TRUE   FALSE

2. Most guys expect girls to kiss them if they spend money on them or give them a little attention.

    TRUE   FALSE

3. Most guys will stop being interested or drop you if you don't give them what they want physically.

    TRUE   FALSE

4. Most guys want you to be interested in what they do but don't care much about girls' interests.

    TRUE   FALSE

5. Most guys could care less if girls are smart or dumb, as long as they're good looking.

TRUE   FALSE

6. Most guys will hang out with friends instead of girls they like (unless the guys are trying to establish the relationship).

TRUE   FALSE

7. Most guys are naturally romantic.

TRUE   FALSE

8. Most guys will brag to other guys about what they do with their girlfriends.

TRUE   FALSE

9. Most guys try too hard to impress girls.

TRUE   FALSE

10. Most guys don't have a clue about how girls think or feel.

TRUE   FALSE

Permission granted to reproduce this talksheet only for use in buyer's own youth group. This page can be downloaded from the Web site for this book:

www.YouthSpecialties.com/store/downloads   code: highway 5
© YouthSpecialties. www.YouthSpecialties.com

What Girls Are Like Talksheet

Please answer the following questions as honestly as you can. When you circle your answers, don't think about a specific girl or only girls who call themselves Christians—think about girls in general.

1. Most girls aren't happy unless they have boyfriends.

TRUE   FALSE

2. Most girls will go out with guys they don't really like if the guys invite them to places the girls really want to go.

TRUE   FALSE

3. When on a date, most girls expect a guy to open doors for them, pull out their chairs for them at the table, and so on.

TRUE   FALSE

4. Most girls have no idea how boring it is for guys to go shopping with them.

TRUE   FALSE

5. Most girls who dress sexy know they're sending a message to guys about what they're willing to do physically.

TRUE   FALSE

6. Most girls will dump guys if other guys with more money come along.

TRUE   FALSE

7. Most girls share their secrets with their friends.

TRUE   FALSE

8. Most girls expect way too much from guys they date in high school.

TRUE   FALSE

9. Most girls worry too much about their weight and their looks.

TRUE   FALSE

10. Most girls have no idea how a guy thinks.

TRUE   FALSE

Permission granted to reproduce this talksheet only for use in buyer's own youth group. This page can be downloaded from the Web site for this book:

www.YouthSpecialties.com/store/downloads   code: highway 5
© YouthSpecialties. www.YouthSpecialties.com

The Perfect Guy

Production Notes: The Perfect Guy

Director: Ryan Pettey

Okay, so I know the "Perfect Guy" doll is cheesy. You've probably seen it in the stores and passed it off as some novelty gift your Aunt Lucy would give to your 80-year-old Grandma Ethel for Christmas. You know, the kind of gift exchange where your aunt gets all excited when your grandma opens it and says something like, "Press the hand, Nana!" Then they look at each other with the "This is so clever!" face, and you spend the rest of the day trying to tune out the constant onslaught of pseudo-charming remarks.

To be honest, my inspiration for this video came from *Seinfeld*. Of the show's recurring jokes, one of my favorites was Jerry's overly picky attitude toward the women he dated. He was always able to find what he considered small imperfections in the character or physical appearance of each potential girlfriend (for example, the woman with "man hands"). I thought it would be funny to base a simple mockumentary around this premise, making fun of the absurdity of it, but also trying to communicate the spiritual parallels associated with perfectionism.

The Perfect Guy is a short comedy that shows the pointlessness of seeking perfection—in us or in others. Only God is perfect; the rest of us fall short. Therefore, demanding perfection in a relationship or from yourself is pointless as well. What seems like perfection in others is only artificial or surface-level. Just look at Mitch—he's plastic! *The Perfect Guy* showcases a vain attempt at finding "Mr. Right."

Transformation 2

the
Covenant

Alternate Routes

 ## Emergent Ministries

Use the *Transformation* video clip to introduce the idea of God's changing work in the lives of all believers. (Note: This is a contemplative video piece and best used in that context.)

 ### Small Group

Focus: God never stops changing those who put their trust in him

Biblical basis: Romans 12:2

Stuff you need: chalkboard or poster board, something to write with, discussion questions, *Transformation* video clip

Getting Started

Write the word METAMORPHOSIS on a chalkboard or poster board. Ask your group:

• Can you give me the definition of this word? How about an example?

• Do you think that what a chameleon does fits the definition of metamorphosis? Why or why not?

• Do you think people really change, or do you think they stay the same and merely camouflage themselves from time to time?

Transition to the film by saying something like this:

Here's a short film essay on this idea of metamorphosis or transformation. Let's take a look at it and see if you can pick up on what's being transformed.

Show the *Transformation* video clip. After it ends, slide into a discussion-driven Bible study by saying something like this:

> Let's take a look at where this idea of transformation comes from in the Bible. While there are many hints about this concept all over Scripture, there's one place where it's the centerpiece concept. Let's turn to Romans 12:2.

Bible Study

Read Romans 12:2 and then ask:

- What does it mean to renew our minds?
- How might the process of mind renewal work?
- What are we being transformed from and what are we being transformed into?
- In what way does faith in Christ change one's outlook on life and on others?
- Suppose somebody says she is a Christian but then never really changes—or she says she has no reason to change—do you think her faith is valid? Why or why not?
- Do you think everyone changes in the same way or in the same areas of life? Why or why not?
- What are some tools God uses to help create a changed perspective in believers?

Wrap Up

Ask your group to consider one area of their lives in which they'd like God to do a "makeover." Close with private prayer, with each person giving God permission to conform him to the image of Jesus.

Middle School

Focus: Lives given to God are changed!

Biblical basis: Acts 7:55-58, 9:1-22, 22:3-5; Galatians 3:27

Stuff you need: paper, pencils, pens, markers, *Transformation* video clip

Getting Started

Tell your students this little story called "The Man with the Ugly Face" (adapted from a tale C.S. Lewis uses in *Mere Christianity*).

> Once upon a time there was a man with an absolutely hideous face. He was so ugly (much uglier than anyone in this room) that children cried out in fright and adults stood gaping. Embarrassed by his own features, the man had a mask crafted. The firm mask showed a face of strong, elegant beauty—quite unlike the face of the one who would wear it.
>
> Every morning without fail, the man with the ugly face got up and put on the beautiful mask. He knew he was pretending and that people who saw him would wonder about the mask; but to him, it was much better than showing them who he really was.
>
> Every day, year in and year out, the man got up in the morning and put the mask on his face.
>
> One morning as he got up and went to fetch his mask, he caught his reflection in the window glass. Dismayed at what he saw, he frantically searched his house for a mirror (which was quite a task, as he'd eliminated most of them years ago, not caring for the image of truth they returned). Upon finding a small hand mirror he gazed in shock—and finally joy at what he saw.

It seems that by putting on the mask year in and year out, his bone and tissue had formed to the mold of that mask, and he was ugly no more. In fact, his face had been transformed into the exact replica of the beautiful mask.

Ask your students to give you suggestions as to what this parable might be about. (Read Galatians 3:27 aloud if they need a hint.)

Transition to the *Transformation* video clip by saying something like this:

> The Bible promises that God will someday transform all believers from what we are now (as ugly as our hearts) into his likeness. The Bible also promises that the transformation begins now. Let's take a look at a short video clip that makes a comment on that incredible change.

▶ *Transformation* Video Clip

After you've played the clip, transition to the Bible study by saying something like this:

> God changes people in big and small ways. Sometimes the changes are going on and you don't even notice them for a long while, and sometimes the changes are dramatic and can't be missed. Let's take a look at one of the most dramatic transformations in the Bible. As we do, remember that as huge as this change was, God was only just starting his work.

Transformation
vol chp pg
05: 02: 25

Bible Study

Pass out pencils and paper to your students. Ask them to work in pairs to create a cartoon strip that chronicles the change and transformation that took place in the life of the apostle Paul. Depending on the size of your group and the time allotted, you can have your small groups work through his entire transformation or assign specific passages in the journey for them to illustrate. Assign the following passages: Acts 7:55-58, 9:1-22, and 22:3-5. When your students are done, ask them to share what they've created and post their work on the wall.

Ask your students—

- Do you think God still transforms people? If so, what does this look like?

- Do you think the transformation continues after we put our trust in Christ? If so, in what ways?

- How can our lives change if we "clothe ourselves with Christ," as the Bible suggests? (Think back to the opening story…)

Wrap Up

Tell your kids—

We know God is in the business of changing people. We've seen what he did with a character like Paul. But not all transformations are huge. Some of them are small. Can you think of one way God has changed you for the better?

Pass out paper, markers, pens, and pencils and ask your students to jot down at least one way they've seen God's transforming power at work.

Ask several willing students to share what they've written.

Close in prayer.

 High School

Focus: God is out to make astonishing changes in our lives

Biblical basis: Matthew 5:21-24, 27-28, 43-47, 6:1, 19-21, 7:1-5; Romans 12:2

Stuff you need: photos of "extreme makeovers" (available online), paper, pencils, *Transformation* video clip

Getting Started

Idea #1: Talk to your students about the idea of transformation by getting a discussion going about various "extreme makeover" television programs. Visit a Web site or two showing before and after photos of these extreme makeovers (just Google the word "makeover" in the image section for some visual examples).

Ask questions such as—

- How many of you have watched an extreme makeover program—when a person or house is transformed into a thing of beauty?

- What do you like or dislike about those programs?

- Would you ever offer yourself for an extreme makeover?

- How extreme a transformation should people allow themselves?

- Are fake body parts (breasts, bottoms, chins, and so on) too much?

- Do you think people who do what Michael Jackson has done to his face, for example, have gone too far?
- Does changing the outside package also transform the inside? Why or why not?
- Do you think it could work the other way around—a person who becomes changed (for either good or bad) on the inside then changes on the outside? Offer any examples of this that you can think of.

Transition to the Bible study by saying something like this:

> It's obvious that people often want to change how they appear, and some will go to great expense and pain to "look good." God is into change as well. It's part of his plan, for those who trust him, to create people of beauty from the inside out. Let's consider what that might look like.

Idea #2: Ask a student who is adept at photography to briefly explain how a black-and-white image shows up on a blank piece of photo paper. (A chemically treated piece of paper is exposed to light of various intensities coming through a negative, which burns the shades of contrast on the paper. The paper is then bathed in a chemical that triggers the transformation.)

Use this as a metaphor for what God does to us. He prepares us with his Holy Spirit when we take our first steps of faith and trust him. God exposes us to his light in order to produce in us what he wants to see displayed, and then he plunges us into situations that help bring out that image. He transforms us from what we were to what he wants us to be.

Transition to the Bible study by saying something like this:

> Those who become Christians and think God isn't out to deeply change them are in for a surprise. Change and transformation are part of a Christian's DNA. Let's consider what that might look like in everyday life.

Bible Study

Idea #1: Read Romans 12:2 to your students from *The Message*: "Don't become so well adjusted to your culture that you fit into it without even thinking. Instead, fix your attention on God. You'll be changed from the inside out. Readily recognize what he wants from you, and quickly respond to it. Unlike the culture around you, always dragging you down to its level of immaturity, God brings the best out of you, develops well-formed maturity in you."

After you've read this passage, show the *Transformation* video clip. Transition to the video by saying something like this:

> This passage gives us the prescription for how God wants our lives to change. Here's a video that offers a creative take on this whole concept. Let's take a minute and see how "transformation" is presented.

After playing the clip, slide into the Bible study by saying something like this:

> One of the facts about the Christian faith is that it's an adventure in change. All those who really walk with Christ will change. Their thoughts, attitudes, and— ultimately—actions are continually

Transformation
vol chp pg
05: 02: 29

being challenged and altered. All of this takes time, and it also takes some thinking. Let's put our minds to work by looking at some of Jesus' radical ideas and considering the transformation those ideas would create in us if we took them to heart.

Break your students into groups of three to four each and assign each group at least one of the following passages: Matthew 5:21-24, 5:27-28, 5:43-47, 6:1, 6:19-21, 7:1-5.

Ask them to find the principle of the kingdom (the way God would have us think and behave) and contrast it with the common mindset on the subject today.

Here's an example of what that might look like:

> Enemies—the kingdom principle is to love and pray for our enemies. (Make sure the students explain what it looks like to love your enemies—it doesn't mean just letting them off the hook for their evil behavior.) The common worldly attitude is to hate, hurt, and defeat our enemies.

Idea #2: Before the start of your group time, arrange to have a small group of men and women come and share one thing that God has transformed in their lives. (You may have to emphasize your time limit if you have more than one or two guests.) Try to get a varied group of stories—some radical, some sublime, some ordinary. Allow time for questions after each guest.

Read Romans 12:2 to your students from *The Message*: "Don't become so well adjusted to your culture that you fit into it without even thinking. Instead, fix your attention on God. You'll be changed from the inside out. Readily recognize what he wants from you, and quickly respond to it. Unlike the culture around you, always dragging you down to its level of immaturity, God brings the best out of you, develops well-formed maturity in you."

Transition to the *Transformation* video clip by saying something like this:

> **Let's see how this idea might be visualized or interpreted on video by watching this clip.**

Show the video clip. Afterward introduce your guests by telling your students something like this:

> **Since God is out to change and transform each of us, I thought it would be interesting for you to meet some real-life examples of what that change and transformation can look like. I have arranged for a few special guests to share with you one important change God has made in each of them. Let's welcome them!**

Encourage students to ask questions during the sharing time.

Wrap Up

Idea #1: Ask your students to share one attitude, idea, or action each that God has changed in them over the last year. You may want to have them tell a friend, write the change down on paper, or invite those willing to speak up to tell the group about it.

Close in prayer.

Idea #2: Tell your students—

> Let's imprint the idea of God's transforming work on our hearts and minds by burning a key passage into our memory banks.

Ask your students to commit Romans 12:2 to memory (from whatever Bible translation you believe is easiest for them to use). Have them practice saying it a few times so you know they've got it down.

Close in prayer.

Production Notes: Transformation

Actor/Editor: Joe Perez

This is what I went through on camera for you guys—literally! Usually, Highway is less literal in its approaches to the ideas we communicate. But this time around, we thought it would be much more poignant to illustrate a transformation process happening before your eyes.

I think the story goes like this: Kevin, one of our writers, had a script ready and loaded but he just needed an actor to pull the trigger. To Highway's benefit, I am a person of many hairstyles, and I switch them like one switches hats. At the time of the filming, I possessed a mop top and was getting tired of it. So I conceded to the idea that every bit of action in my life (and for that matter, a Highway employee's life) could be filmed and turned into some sort of visual metaphor for use in ministry. I announced that I would be cutting my hair and that we should do something with it. Travis pulled out a camera, some lights, and a pair of scissors and then told me to start cutting. I edited the piece together—and you have *Transformation*.

The Good Pens 3

Gulp.

Alternate Routes

 Emergent Ministries

The Good Pens is a multilayered, fascinating, and humorous little parable that can be used to illustrate temptation or the guilt that comes from sin—just to name a couple of possible topics. Weave it carefully into a message, and you'll have a great teaching tool.

 Small Group

Focus: Guilt is the unwanted paycheck of sin

Biblical basis: Psalm 38:1-22, 39:1, 51:1-17; Proverbs 1:10, 6:6-11, 10:4-5, 30:9; Luke 5:8; Ephesians 4:27; 1 Timothy 6:9-10; James 1:14; 1 Peter 5:8-9

Stuff you need: pencils, *The Good Pens* video clip, copies of the How Did I Get Here? Talksheet (page 44) (a free download is available atwww.YouthSpecialties.com/store/downloads   code: highway 5)

Getting Started

Watch *The Good Pens* video clip right out of the gate. It's a great opener for discussion. Before you show it, ask the group to be prepared to give you feedback on the clip's message.

Ask—What is the message of this clip? Allow time for people to contribute their ideas based on what they saw in the clip, and then transition to the Bible study by saying something like this:

> **Let's take a couple of those ideas and examine them more deeply.**

Bible Study

Since *The Good Pens* video clip hits a few topics, use the How Did I Get Here? Talksheet on page 44 to break up your discussion into areas such as:

Idleness

(Look up these passages for some help: Psalm 39:1; Proverbs 6:6-11, 10:4-5; Ephesians 4:27.) Notice that boredom and idleness gave the main character time to poke around the supply center? Discuss idleness and a lack of caution by asking—

- Can having too much time on your hands be spiritually dangerous?
- What Old Testament king got in trouble when he had too much idle time? (King David, who should have been out with his troops instead of messing around on a rooftop with a married woman.)

Temptation

(Look up these passages for some help: Proverbs 1:10, 30:9; 1 Timothy 6:9-10; James 1:14; 1 Peter 5:8-9.)

Ask—

- When you're tempted, is that sin?
- Can temptation always be avoided? If yes, how?
- Can we put ourselves in situations that make temptation more likely? Give an example.

Guilt

(Look up these passages for some help: Psalm 38:1-22, 51:1-17; Luke 5:8.)

Ask—

- In what ways does guilt affect you?

- Does it stop joy, growth in Christ, or the ability to serve him well?

- Can you offer an example from a dumb thing you did at a younger age (such as stealing a toy) that produced guilt and shame in you that far outweighed whatever "gain" you received from your actions?

- Why do you think many of us participate in activities that we pretty much know will make us feel rotten and guilty afterward?

- How do we get rid of guilt? What can we do to extinguish it?

- Can we be forgiven and still feel twinges of guilt for what we've done?

Wrap Up

Ask the group to work in pairs to see if they can create a motto or moral for the subject of temptation, sin, and guilt. It can be humorous or serious, as long as it sums up a biblical perspective on those subjects. Allow the groups to work for a few minutes, then each pair can share what they've written.

Close in prayer.

Middle School

Focus: The misery and reality of guilt

Biblical basis: Mark 14:66-72; John 21:1-23; 1 John 1:9

Stuff you need: a car battery, pencils, paper, *The Good Pens* video clip

Getting Started

Bring in a car battery or, better yet, take your kids to the parking lot and open the hood of your car.

Ask—

- Why do you have to be careful when handling a car battery or jump-starting a car's battery using cables? (Batteries can explode or leak)
- What's in a battery that's so dangerous? (Acid)
- What happens if you splatter acid on your shirt or pants? (It eats right through clothing)
- What happens if acid touches skin? (It burns flesh)

Transition to the Bible study by saying something like this:

> **God has designed us to react strongly and negatively when we do wrong. That reaction is called "guilt." In a lot of ways, guilt is very much like acid—in time, it'll eat right through whatever defenses you put in front of it, and then it comes after you!**

▶ *The Good Pens* Video Clip

Transition to *The Good Pens* clip by telling your group—

> Let's take a look at a great little video clip that cleverly shows us how uncomfortable it is to live with guilt.

Roll into the Bible study by pointing out that there are many examples in Scripture that parallel this clip.

The Good Pens

vol chp pg
05: 03: 37

Bible Study

Direct your students to Mark 14:66-72 (Peter chickens out when asked to acknowledge Christ) and John 21:1-23 (Jesus reinstates Peter). Ask them to read the passages and then work in pairs to come up with cartoon-like "angel and devil" dialogue that might have gone on in Peter's head as he wrestled through his fears and feelings in both passages.

You may want to prime your students by giving them places to begin, such as:

- Peter follows Jesus at a distance and is warming himself by the fire when a servant girl asks, "Aren't you one of his followers?" POOF! An angel appears on Peter's shoulder and a devil appears on his other shoulder. "Hey!" said the angel...

- Peter, in tears, can't get away from the angel or devil on his shoulders. They're telling him...

- After the resurrection, Jesus approaches Peter. The angel and devil, still on his shoulders, tell him...

Have your students read their dialogues with one student taking the voice of the angel and the other the voice of the devil.

After all the students have had a chance to read their creative interpretations, ask them to do the exercise again—only this time using a temptation that might be common to Christians their age. Before they begin, ask—

- What would the two voices be saying to those people?

- If Christians failed to do what was right, what would the voices say?

Ask them to read back their examples.

Wrap Up

Ask—What's the easiest way to avoid guilt, and what should we do if we find ourselves guilty?

Close by reading 1 John 1:9. Invite your students to unload the burden of guilt they might be carrying by spending some time in prayer with their dialogue partners from the Bible study activity.

High School

Focus: Dealing with temptation and guilt

Biblical basis: Genesis 4:3-15, 37:27-35, 45:1-47; Psalm 19:13, 32:1-11, 46:1, 51:1-13; Proverbs 28:13; Hosea 6:1-3; Matthew 2:1-16, 4:17, 14:3-11, 26:47-50; Mark 14:66-72; John 18:28–19:42; James 5:16; 1 John 1:8-10

Stuff you need: paper, pencils, markers, scissors, *The Good Pens* video clip, copies of Dragging the Weight Talksheet (page 45) (a free download is available at www.YouthSpecialties.com/store/downloads code: highway 5)

Getting Started

Idea #1: Ask your students—What kind of guilt is the hardest to carry? For example, if you were fiddling with your cell phone while driving your car and hit a little kid? What if you gave a friend bad advice and it screwed up his life for good?

▶ *The Good Pens* Video Clip

Transition to the video clip by saying something like this:

The Good Pens
vol chp pg
05: 03: 39

It doesn't take something really nasty happening to get a good case of guilt. Let's take a look at a fun example.

Show *The Good Pens* clip.

Idea #2: Watch *The Good Pens* clip right off the bat. Then ask your students if they've ever felt guilty about something they did when they were kids. Let someone share the details. Then transition to the Bible study by saying something like this:

> **Guilt is one of those horrible bits of baggage that comes with giving into temptation. Let's take a look at this idea in the Bible.**

Bible Study

Idea #1: Give your students some paper, markers, and scissors. Ask them to work in pairs to create a "Guilt Trip Award" to bestow upon a person or group from the Bible who most likely suffered significant guilt. Have your students take turns reading aloud the following passages and then choose who gets the prize:

- Cain (Genesis 4:3-15)
- Joseph's brothers (Genesis 37:27-35, 45:1-47)
- Herod, King of Judah (Matthew 2:1-16)
- Herod, Tetrarch of Galilee (Matthew 14:3-11)
- Judas (Matthew 26:47-50)
- Peter (Mark 14:66-72)
- Pilate (John 18:28–19:42)

Idea #2: Tell your students—

We all do things that are guaranteed to make us feel shame and guilt; those feelings are as important to our souls as pain is to our bodies. Pain and guilt both warn us that something's wrong that needs our attention. And while you may not have any medical skills to stop the pain, if you're a Christian, you have spiritual skills to help you deal with the guilt that results from your bad choices and actions—or even from someone else's. Let's read the following passages and see if we can apply what we've discovered to typical situations in our lives. Keep in mind that in addition to the spiritual help we can give, some people need to be guided to caring adult professionals as part of the healing process.

Break your students into groups of three or four. Pass out copies of the Dragging the Weight Talksheet (page 45) (a free download is available at www.YouthSpecialties.com/store/downloads code: highway 5) and something to write with. Assign each group a case study to read and respond to. Or post the Scripture references (Psalm 19:13; Psalm 46:1; Psalm 51:1-13; Proverbs 28:13; Hosea 6:1-3; Matthew 4:17; James 5:16; 1 John 1:8-10) where your students can see them and then read the case studies aloud so they can come up with suggestions for relieving the person's guilt in each scenario. If you choose not to use the student guides, you'll need to pass out paper and pencils so the students can write down their suggestions.

When the groups are finished, have someone from each group read her group's case study and response. Allow others to interject regarding what they've heard or would do.

Case Studies:

Your friend confides in you that she is feeling really terrible because of something she's been doing. You have a chance to show your friend a way out of her misery. What do you say? Be prepared to share your solutions with the whole group.

Jeannie comes to you in tears and confides that she had an abortion a year ago. At the time, she didn't think much about it—the fear of being pregnant in high school overwhelmed her. Now she can't seem to get it out of her mind. The guilt and shame are stalking her. What kind of help can you offer her?

Zach was messing around in the garage and accidentally scratched his father's brand-new car. His dad didn't notice it right away and then assumed someone in a parking lot did it. His dad gave a long monologue about the kind of people who would do something like that and not even have the courtesy to acknowledge it, leave a note, and offer to help get it fixed. Zach is feeling guilty for not telling his dad—but fearful as well, especially since he didn't confess right away. How can you help Zach?

Matt has been looking at porn on the Internet. He feels miserable about his lack of self-control and fearful that someone in his family will discover what he's been doing. He wants to stop. How can you help him?

Malia lied to her best friend. She may be able to get away with the lie, but her conscience is gnawing at her. She's not only fearful that she'll lose her friend if she confesses, but also worries that she'll lose her friend if she says nothing and is later found out. What kind of advice do you offer?

Sandee went to a party with some friends. Her friends started drinking heavily and were pretty toasted by the time they decided to go home. Sandee, who hadn't been drinking, decided not to drive home with her friends and instead caught a ride home with someone else who hadn't been drinking. Her friends were killed that night when they ran a stop sign and plowed into a huge truck. Sandee feels guilty and responsible for their deaths. She thinks she should have forced them to let her drive or should have called the cops or something. What do you say that can help her?

Don was on the football team. During a game he tackled another player who broke his neck as a result of their collision. Don is torn up with guilt. What do you say to him?

Allegra cheated on a final exam. Nobody knows but her, yet she feels rotten about it. Now she confides in you. What do you advise?

Wrap Up

Idea #1: Ask your students to take a moment for some self-reflection to see if they're carrying any guilt for unconfessed sin. In a time of silence, invite them to make things right with God and, if necessary, pray about how to make things right with those they may have wronged.

Idea #2: Close by reading together Psalm 32:1-11, David's wonderful prayer seeking God's forgiveness. Invite those students who may need to clear their souls to make this their personal prayer as well.

How Did I Get Here? Talksheet

Now that you've seen the goofy parable *The Good Pens*, try coming up with some of your best answers to the following questions about what's often swirled in with the process of sin: idleness, temptation, and guilt.

Idleness
(Look up these passages for some help: Psalm 39:1; Proverbs 6:6-11, 10:4-5; Ephesians 4:27.)

- Can having too much time on your hands be spiritually dangerous?
- What Old Testament king got in trouble when he had too much idle time?

Temptation
(Look up these passages for some help: Proverbs 1:10, 30:9; 1 Timothy 6:9-10; James 1:14; 1 Peter 5:8-9.)

- When you're tempted, is that sin?
- Can temptation always be avoided? If yes, how?
- Can we put ourselves in situations that make temptation more likely? Give an example.

Guilt
(Look up these passages for some help: Psalm 38:1-22, 51:1-17; Luke 5:8.)

- In what ways does guilt affect you?
- Does it stop joy, growth in Christ, or the ability to serve him well?
- Can you offer an example from a dumb thing you did at a younger age (such as stealing a toy) that produced guilt and shame in you that far outweighed whatever "gain" you received from your actions?
- Why do you think many of us participate in activities that we pretty much know will make us feel rotten and guilty afterward?

- How do we get rid of guilt? What can we do to extinguish it?
- Can we be forgiven and still feel twinges of guilt for what we've done?

Permission granted to reproduce this talksheet only for use in buyer's own youth group. This page can be downloaded from the Web site for this book:

www.YouthSpecialties.com/store/downloads   code: highway 5
© YouthSpecialties. www.YouthSpecialties.com

Dragging the Weight Talksheet

Take turns reading aloud the following passages—

- Psalm 19:13
- Psalm 46:1
- Psalm 51:1-13
- Proverbs 28:13
- Hosea 6:1-3
- Matthew 4:17
- James 5:16
- 1 John 1:8-10

They'll help prepare you to offer wise counsel to those who might find themselves in situations similar to those in the following case studies.

Case Studies:

Your friend confides in you that she is feeling really terrible because of something she's been doing. You have a chance to show your friend a way out of her misery. What do you say? Be prepared to share your solutions with the whole group.

The Good Pens

vol chp pg
05: 03: 45

Jeannie comes to you in tears and confides that she had an abortion a year ago. At the time, she didn't think much about it—the fear of being pregnant in high school overwhelmed her. Now she can't seem to get it out of her mind. The guilt and shame are stalking her. What kind of help can you offer her?

Zach was messing around in the garage and accidentally scratched his father's brand-new car. His dad didn't notice it right away and then assumed someone in a parking lot did it. His dad gave a long monologue about the kind of people who would do something like that and not even have the courtesy to acknowledge it, leave a note, and offer to help get it fixed. Zach is feeling guilty for not telling his dad—but fearful as well, especially since he didn't confess right away. How can you help Zach?

Matt has been looking at porn on the Internet. He feels miserable about his lack of self-control and fearful that someone in his family will discover what he's been doing. He wants to stop. How can you help him?

Malia lied to her best friend. She may be able to get away with the lie, but her conscience is gnawing at her. She's not only fearful that she'll lose her friend if she confesses, but also worries that she will lose her friend if she says nothing and is later found out. What kind of advice do you offer?

Sandee went to a party with some friends. Her friends started drinking heavily and were pretty toasted by the time they decided to go home. Sandee, who hadn't been drinking, decided not to drive home with her friends and instead caught a ride home with someone else who hadn't been drinking. Her friends were killed that night when they ran a stop sign and plowed into a huge truck. Sandee feels guilty and responsible for their deaths. She thinks she should have forced them to let her drive or should have called the cops or something. What do you say that can help her?

Don was on the football team. During a game he tackled another player who broke his neck as a result of their collision. Don is torn up with guilt. What do you say to him?

Allegra cheated on a final exam. Nobody knows but her, yet she feels rotten about it. Now she confides in you. What do you advise?

Permission granted to reproduce this talksheet only for use in buyer's own youth group. This page can be downloaded from the Web site for this book:

www.YouthSpecialties.com/store/downloads code: highway 5
© YouthSpecialties. www.YouthSpecialties.com

Production Notes: The Good Pens

Writer/Director: Kevin Marks

As students, you are full of life, vigor, and endless possibilities. The paths that spread out before you are wide open, and only God knows the swaths of color you will paint on the world. That being said, about 75.6 percent of you will end up working dead-end office jobs. But take heart! I was once employed with a dead-end office job as well, and now look at me—a successful writer and director for Highway Video.

The Good Pens was inspired by an actual event that took place while I was working at one of my very first dead-end office jobs. Since I was one of the younger folks on the team, they thought I'd be good at "recruiting," which in dead-end-office-job-speak translates as, "making so many photocopies of résumés that your very existence shrivels into oblivion." Our copy machine was located in our office supply room and as the machine whizzed on its infinite loop of duplication, I would organize the office supplies on the shelves for something to do. (I have a weird, as-yet-undiagnosed obsession with having things "tidy.") One day I was checking out these pens when a coworker came in and gave me a hard time about trying to steal them. (He was only kidding, of course. He worked a dead-end office job like me and was just trying to spice up his life a little!)

The Good Pens

vol chp pg
05: 03: 47

This scene was basically ripped off from a Woody Allen film called *Annie Hall*, which is probably rated R so I can't recommend it here. Anyway, there's a great scene in which these two characters go out on their first date and subtitles are indicating their true feelings—the implication being, What if we went through life like that? What if the whole world knew how we really felt? Chances are, we might be pretty ashamed. Lucky for us, God's grace is sufficient.

Speaking of grace, we filmed *The Good Pens* at Vocent Solutions in Mountain View, California. We used so much lighting and video equipment that we blew many of their circuit breakers, but they didn't seem to mind. Thanks Vocent. (And thanks for the pens.)

Christen Cross Journey Story   4

Small Group

Focus: Learning to be honest and put away false fronts

Biblical basis: Psalm 32:8, 42:5, 94:191; Mark 14:38; John 14:1, 27; Romans 15:1; 1 Thessalonians 5:11, 14; James 5:16

Stuff you need: paper, pencils, *Christen Cross Journey Story* video clip

Getting Started

Ask the group if they know the origin of the word hypocrite. Allow a few stabs at the answer, and if no one comes up with one, explain that the word came from ancient Greek actors who carried large masks (to be visible in large amphitheaters) with facial expressions indicating the type of characters they played. Since the true expressions of the mask holders may have been considerably different from the masks' expressions, the term hypocrite became slang for those who pretend to be who they aren't.

Transition to the *Christen Cross Journey Story* video clip by saying something like this:

> **Many of us hide what we're really thinking and dealing with deep inside. Let's take a look at a video clip about a young woman who talks about the results of living that way.**

Show the *Christen Cross Journey Story* video clip. Then transition to the Bible study by saying something like this:

> **One of the key ingredients to Christian growth is the willingness to be transparent and open with others about our fears, weaknesses, and struggles. This isn't always easy, as we're often**

ashamed or embarrassed to admit those sorts of things, fearing others will think less of us. So it's sometimes easier to put on the mask. Let's consider a few examples of how God might have us respond to people who are struggling to live the Christian life among us.

 ## Bible Study

Pass out paper and pencils for note taking. Ask the group to break off into smaller groups and create real-life scenarios or examples of people in Christian groups who refuse to admit they have problems, instead they "play Christian" while they're truly struggling inside. Ask the smaller groups to share their examples with everyone.

Tell your group—

> These examples are common problems. The big question is what can we do about them? Let's see what advice we can wring from Scripture, both for the people who are in the middle of the struggle, as well as for their Christian friends.

Then ask the group to read and draw ideas from the following passages: Psalm 32:8, 42:5, 94:191; Mark 14:38; John 14:1, 27; Romans 15:1; 1 Thessalonians 5:11, 14; and James 5:16. When they've had enough time, ask—

> Based on these passages and the real-life situations you created, what advice would you offer? Whom would you advise—the person with the struggle or that person's friends?

Wrap Up

Pass out paper and pencils. Invite people who are struggling to simply write their names and contact numbers on the papers; everyone else should write the names of friends who are struggling so the group will remember to pray for them and make themselves available to their friends this week. Everyone should fold their papers in half, and then you should collect them. Make sure to contact, as soon as possible, those people who responded by writing down their phone numbers.

Close in prayer.

 ## Middle School

Focus: Avoiding putting on masks

Biblical basis: Matthew 7:4-6, 15:1-9; Luke 6:46; Acts 5:1-10

Stuff you need: sheets of cardstock, markers, glue sticks, magazines, Popsicle sticks, edible prizes, *Christen Cross Journey Story* video clip

Getting Started

Invite your students to come up with "facts" about themselves that are either true or fictional—as long as the false stories are so far-fetched (or seemingly far-fetched) that the group will have a really hard time figuring out if they're true or false. Vote on each "fact" and count the votes. Then ask each student whether or not the story is true. If more people voted incorrectly than correctly, the student has stumped the group! Award that student a small, edible prize and go on to the next kid.

Transition to the video clip by saying something like this:

> Many of us live out some kind of fiction about ourselves as fact—or vice versa. We pretend we're doing just fine when inside we're fearful, angry, weak, ashamed, and so on. Let's take a look of a real-life example of a young woman who spent her teen years living in that kind of world.

Show the *Christen Cross Journey Story* video clip. Afterward, ask—

- What was Christen's problem?
- How did she handle it?
- What should she have done?
- She says she can spot kids in her youth group who are going through the same things she went through—how does she help them?

Transition to the Bible study by saying something like this:

> Let's take a look at some biblical examples of what happens when people try to live out lies.

Bible Study

Pass out materials for your students to use to make masks. (They can be as simple as sheets of cardstock with Popsicle sticks and a pile of magazines.) Describe the idea of a hypocrite to your students—the word came from ancient Greek actors who carried large masks (in order to be visible to audiences in large amphitheaters) with facial expressions that indicated the type of characters they played. Since the true expressions of the mask holders may have been considerably different from the masks' expressions, the term hypocrite became slang for those who pretend to be who they are not.

Divide into groups of three to four students each and ask each group to come up with a double-sided mask—the face the person is presenting and the face of the real person. Have them scour magazines for images to use (or draw the facial images themselves), as well as the following Scriptures—Matthew 7:4-6, 15:1-9; Luke 6:46; Acts 5:1-10. Then have them create masks to represent the ones that are worn most often by kids their age. Point out that not all the masks people wear are designed to boost their pride; some are designed to hide their pain—as in Christen's story.

After the exercise, ask your students: Why do you think we put up false fronts? Is this dangerous?

Wrap Up

Ask your students to prayerfully select one person with whom they will commit to being completely honest. Encourage your students to select an older and wiser person—someone who will give them good advice and be able to help them if help is needed. Encourage students who feel they need to get things off their chests to make sure to go to that person this week.

Close in prayer.

High School

Focus: Learning to be honest and helping those who are unwilling to face their pain

Biblical basis: Isaiah 29:15; Matthew 23:27; Acts 5:1-10, 8:13-23

Stuff you need: magazine ads, paper, pencils, a resource counselor willing to share with your group, *Christen Cross Journey Story* video clip

Getting Started

Idea #1: Start a discussion about false advertising by bringing in some magazine ads that promise more than they give. Post them around the room and ask your students to vote for the ad that presents the biggest con job.

Then discuss the false advertising we do for ourselves. For instance, some women use wigs, false eyelashes, makeup, Botox, and plastic surgery in order to look completely different—is this false advertising? Some men use hairpieces, hair dye, and plastic surgery as well—is this false advertising? How about the way some people act and present themselves?

Transition to the *Christen Cross Journey Story* video clip by pointing out that some of us put on false fronts in order to hide things that really bother them—though not necessarily out of vanity or to seem better than others, but to protect themselves. Let your students know that this video is an example of a person who lived a lie to hide her pain.

Show the *Christen Cross Journey Story*. Discuss the various elements in the story—hiding feelings, self-destruction, and so on. Then transition to Idea #1 of the Bible study section (further on) by saying something like this:

We all know that wearing masks is not uncommon. The Bible is full of examples of that kind of thing. Let's take a moment and check out a few more examples.

Idea #2: This opener is designed to work with Idea #2 of the Bible study section (further on). Read your students the results of the following survey and ask their thoughts.

The following are recent figures published by the Centers for Disease Control (CDC) as part of its Youth Risk Behavior Surveillance System (YRBSS). The stats were derived from a national, school-based survey of 10,904 high school students in ninth through twelfth grades. (For more information see CDC, Youth Risk Behavior Surveillance—United States, 1995. MMWR; 45 [No. SS-4], 1-86, 1996.) During the 12 months preceding the survey:

- 24.1 percent of students thought seriously about attempting suicide.

- 17.7 percent of students made a specific plan to attempt suicide.

- 8.7 percent of students attempted suicide.

- 2.8 percent of students made a suicide attempt that resulted in an injury, poisoning, or overdose that required medical attention.

Among all ages, suicide claims more American lives than homicide.

Tell your students:

While these percentages change from year to year, the fact remains that a whole lot of young people are struggling with self-destructive thoughts and feelings—and many of those students are in our churches. Let's take a look at a short video where a young woman explains the story of her struggle.

Play the *Christen Cross Journey Story* video clip. Comment after the video—

> Christen says she can spot kids who are like she was. But many of us don't see the signs and maybe wouldn't know what to do if we did. Today we have invited a guest who can help us with that.

Transition to Bible study Idea #2.

Bible Study

Idea #1: Divide your students into groups of four to five each and assign each group at least one of the following Bible passages—Isaiah 29:15; Matthew 23:27; Acts 5:1-10; Acts 8:13-23. Then ask each group to read the passage or account and create a modernized skit based on the passage's theme. The skit can be a pantomime or have spoken dialogue. Give your kids time to work on this short skit and then ask them to perform it for the rest of the group.

Idea #2: Invite a professional Christian counselor to come to your group and discuss how your students can help their friends who are doing self-destructive things. Make sure to ask the counselor to point out warning signs to be aware of and to use as much Scripture as possible to augment the discussion. Allow your students to ask questions.

Wrap Up

Invite your students to spend some time in private introspection to consider whether the images they present to others are who they really are. During this time of prayer, invite students to commit to being honest with another older, wiser person.

Production Notes: Christen Cross Journey Story

Director: Will Canon

There's a lot of back-story to this piece, which ended up being about four minutes long. A lot of the details were cut, but I'll try to explain a little bit of where the story came from, why I wanted to tell it, as well as offer some information that I hope you'll find useful.

I don't think you can take a life and a story like Christen's and extract an easily digestible point to pass on to kids. You can say, "Don't do this," but I think Christen probably heard people say those exact things to her, and she still went down a difficult path.

It's easy to say Christen made bad choices. No one would argue that. She definitely made some terrible decisions. But what's interesting to me is asking why Christen made those decisions. What was going on underneath the surface? The choices Christen made were symptoms of a much larger problem. What struck me the most while listening to her was the lack of support and foundation Christen had around her. She wasn't a bad kid, but she had so little in the way of guidance that the door was open for her to make some of those really harmful decisions. Christen didn't have good role models around her to influence her decisions in positive ways. She probably never had a chance.

I have a friend who works in childcare. One day while we were talking, he explained the different ways children need structure provided for them. He said that when kids have structure, they could spend their energy learning, being creative, and doing their homework—that sort of thing. But if no structure is provided, then their energy has to go into creating structure for themselves. If kids are creating their own structure, they don't have the time and energy to learn, to be creative, to do the developmental things most of us do while growing up because we had that structure provided for us. It's the difference between thriving in life and just surviving it. Christen did her best just to survive.

She didn't have anyone telling her that she shouldn't stay out all night. She didn't have anyone there to listen to her, someone with whom she could share what was going on inside of her. Christen started taking pills and cutting herself in seventh grade to get someone's—anyone's—attention. When no one noticed, she went in an even worse direction. She tried to commit suicide on several occasions. She dropped out of high school and experimented with some pretty heavy drugs. Everything we tell kids in youth groups not to do, Christen did.

It's been a tough lesson to learn that the decisions you make in junior high and high school can affect you for the next 10 to 15 years—even longer. It's not meant to scare kids, but Christen's story should serve as a cautionary tale to students and, more importantly, to youth workers and other adults about the roads their kids can travel down if they don't have caring adults involved in their lives.

While sitting down with Christen, she communicated that she really wants kids who are struggling to know they aren't alone. She wants them to know there are people out there who've been through what they are going through, and they are loved. One of the most important things Christen shared with me was that when she was at her lowest point, she prayed to God and asked, "God, are you there? Do you still love me?" And it was a crucial moment for her because she realized that he did.

Christen walks around, as we all do, with some heavy baggage that is made lighter by God's grace.

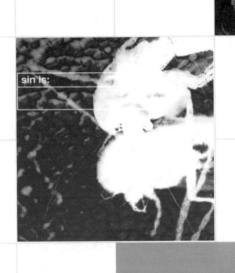

sin is:

The Sin Vibe   5

Alternate Routes

General Church and Emergent Ministries Use

Show the video clip *The Sin Vibe* as a prelude to a message that discusses how sin brings disaster to our lives. The clip's sober tone is ideal as a reflective or meditative supplement.

With a little tinkering, *The Sin Vibe* can also prove a great teaching tool for the Easter season or any other time you're focusing on Christ's sacrifice for our sins.

Small Group

Focus: Sin is a trap from which only Christ can free us

Biblical basis: Romans 7:24-25, 8:1; 1 John 1:9

Stuff you need: credit card, mousetrap, pencils, paper, *The Sin Vibe* video clip, copies of the Talk to Me! Talksheet (page 75) (a free download is available at www.YouthSpecialties.com/store/downloads code: highway 5)

Getting Started

Get your group rolling with a discussion that leads into the idea of sin's attractiveness and ultimate wretchedness. Here are a few ideas to help get you started.

Idea #1: Ask your group—

- Do you have a credit card?
- Do you want one?

- What's the positive side of having a credit card?
- What's the downside of having a credit card?
- What happens if you only make your minimum payment but keep charging?
- What happens to your interest if you miss payments?
- Did you know the average college senior has six credit cards and is nearly $4,000 in debt?
- What is so attractive about credit cards that people will allow themselves to get so deep in debt that it takes them years to get out from under it?
- Are there parallels between credit cards and sin? If so, what are they?

Idea #2: Ask your group—

- Have you—or someone you know well—ever jumped into something impulsively or without researching it ahead of time, only to regret the decision later? (Let someone from the group offer an example. Then ask these follow-up questions.)
- What makes those kinds of "opportunities" so attractive?
- Why can't people detect the landmines surrounding situations that seemed like "such a good idea" at the time?
- Did anyone offer you any warnings? If so, why didn't you heed them?
- Can we end up in sin through the same kind of process?
- Why does sin seem so attractive to us?

Idea #3: Bring in a mousetrap and a bit of cheese. Discuss the workings and results of a mousetrap by asking:

- Wood, metal, and cheese. If you were the average mouse, there's nothing unusual about any of these elements—so what makes the trap deadly?

- Are there parallels between the mousetrap and sin?

- If it's true that the bait isn't the problem (the bait being, in and of itself, harmless) but it's the context in which the bait is found (a deadly trap), does that hold any meaning for our problem with sin? Give some examples.

Transition to the Bible study by saying something like this:

> **All Christians struggle with (and are sometimes overwhelmed by) sin—the disobedience of or disregard for God's Word or ways. Let's take a look at this difficult subject as the Bible spells it out.**

Bible Study

Toss around these discussion questions with your group. You may want to prepare the answers for some of these questions in advance, as they may spark a lot of discussion.

(You can also download these questions from the Talk to Me! Talksheet (page 75) at www.YouthSpecialties.com/store/downloads   code: highway 5).

- How would you define the word *sin*?

- Can sin be something you don't do? Explain.

- Are all sins equal? Explain your answer.

- Why do you think we do things that we clearly know are wrong?

- Why does sin often seem fun? What's deceptive about this?

- Is everyone attracted to the same kinds of sins? Why or why not?
- Do people who couldn't care less about God know that they're sinners, too? Why or why not?
- What happens to us when we sin?
- What role does the Holy Spirit play when we sin?
- What does being caught in a nasty sin do to a person?
- Offer examples of sins that are against man and God, and examples of sins that are only against God.
- What happens to us when we refuse to admit our sins?
- Are there sins that don't harm anyone but the people committing them?

▸ *The Sin Vibe* Video Clip

Transition to the video clip by saying something like this:

> **This short video gives a pretty good summary of the final paycheck that sin delivers. Let's take a look at it.**

Show The Sin Vibe and then discuss the one thing that can break sin's grip and misery: Christ's sacrifice on the cross. Ask—

> This film lets us know in no uncertain terms the terrible consequences of sin. But is there anything (or anyone) you can think of that has defeated sin?
> (Point the group to Romans 7:24-25, 8:1.)

What can we do to break the chains of sin?
(Point the group to 1 John 1:9.)

Wrap Up

Ask your group to come up with a symbol or logo idea to symbolize Christ defeating sin on the cross. (Some may note that the cross itself is that symbol, which is true, but encourage them to think outside the box, too.) Brainstorm a few different ideas and invite your group to create pencil sketches. If one or more members are adept at graphics, you may want to ask that person or those persons to take one or two of the designs and polish them up for the group. You can use the designs for logos, T-shirts, and so on.

Close in prayer and thank God for defeating sin—including the stuff that so easily gets to us.

 ## Middle School

Focus: Considering the consequences of sin helps us avoid sin

Biblical basis: Joshua 6:18, 7:1-28; John 1:9

Stuff you need: dirty trashcan, bottle or can of soda, large cup, paper, pencils, *The Sin Vibe* video clip, copies of the Talk to Me! Talksheet (page 75) (a free download is available at www.YouthSpecialties.com/store/downloads code: highway 5)

Getting Started

Use this little object lesson to help your students understand that sin is gross. Have a can or bottle of soda, a dirty trashcan, and a large cup ready to go. Ask your students if any of them would like a soda. Pick one volunteer and invite the student to come up and get it from you—choose a student who doesn't typically enjoy or participate in gross stuff (or takes all sorts of dares). Then dump out the trashcan's contents, open the can or bottle of soda, pour the soda into the trashcan, swish the liquid around a few times, and pour the soda into the large cup. Hand the cup to the student.

Chances are good that the once-thirsty kid will no longer want the soda. Ask the student: What's wrong? There's only a little bit of trash in the soda—what if I strain out the big pieces? Will you drink it then?

Naturally, most kids will have nothing to do with the polluted drink and will be grossed out by any nut that actually drinks the stuff. Transition to the lesson by saying something like this:

> Just as we're disgusted at the thought of polluting our bodies with the trash-infested drink, we also should be disgusted if we pollute our hearts and minds by swimming around in the pollution of sin. Let's take a look at the deadly results of not being careful about how we live.

 ## Bible Study

(Before plunging into the Bible study, make sure you've read Joshua 6 and are familiar with the story of Jericho.) Before breaking your students into groups, briefly summarize for them the background material before jumping into the story of Achan and his disobedience.

Break your students into groups of three or four

and ask them to read Joshua 6:18 and 7:1-28. Then assign each small group a role in a courtroom drama. Depending on the size of your group, you can make assignments in this manner:

- Have the members of one group be the key players in this story (Joshua, Achan, and so on).
- Have the members of one group be the judge and courtroom personnel.
- Have the members of one group be the prosecution.
- Have the members of one group be the defense lawyers.
- Have the remainder of the groups be the jury.

While your kids are working out their roles, set up the youth room to look like a courtroom. For the hearing, "try" Achan using the Bible passage as the basis for law and evidence. (You don't have to execute the poor kid who is Achan, though—just sentence him.) Your kids will show how much of the story they understand by their performances.

After the courtroom drama, assemble your students and ask them to draw out one of the following questions (already printed, cut, and placed inside a container) and—after thinking about it for a few minutes—give their best answers. (You can also download these questions from the Talk to Me! (page 75) at www.YouthSpecialties.com/store/downloads code: highway 5.) Feel free to add to these questions or edit them any way you see fit.

- How would you define the word *sin*?
- Can sin be something you don't do? Explain.
- Are all sins equal? Explain your answer.

- Why do you think we do things that we clearly know are wrong?
- Why does sin often seem fun? What's deceptive about this?
- Are all people attracted to the same kinds of sins? Why or why not?
- Do people who couldn't care less about God know that they're sinners, too? Why or why not?
- What happens to us when we sin?
- What role does the Holy Spirit play when we sin?
- What does being caught in a nasty sin do to a person?
- Offer examples of sins that are against man and God, and examples of sins that are only against God.
- What happens to us when we refuse to admit our sins?
- Are there kinds of sins that don't harm anyone but the people committing them?

Have your students kick back their answers and then use what they say as a basis for a discussion about sin, temptation, repentance, and forgiveness.

▶ *The Sin Vibe* Video Clip

Transition to *The Sin Vibe* video clip by saying something like this:

> Achan ended up getting nothing but trouble because of his disobedience. And his actions created misery for lots of others as well. Here's a short video clip that probably would've expressed well the feelings of everyone involved in this

The Sin Vibe
vol chp pg
05: 05: 69

story—and in stories repeated over and over again to this very day. Let's take a look at it, remembering that it's very easy to slip into similar kinds of disobedience against God in our own lives.

Show *The Sin Vibe* clip.

Wrap Up

Close with a clear gospel presentation, inviting students who've never come to grips with their sin to erase it by putting their faith and trust in Christ. Invite Christian kids to ask for forgiveness (1 John 1:9) and get their spiritual lives back in order. Close in prayer.

High School

Focus: The paycheck for sin is never worth the investment

Biblical basis: Joshua 7:1-26; 1 Samuel 2:22-25, 29, 3:11-14; 2 Samuel 11:2-27, 12:1-23; Psalm 38:1-22; Matthew 6:2-8, 16-18, 15:1-9, 23:2-33; Mark 10:17-22; Luke 15:11-32, 16:19-31; John 8; Acts 5:1-11; Romans 6:23, 7:24-25; 1 Corinthians 1:12-16, 5:1-5; James 2:1-4

Stuff you need: rotten meat or eggs, airtight container, mushrooms, more mushrooms (or photos of them) labeled TOADSTOOLS, *The Sin Vibe* video clip

Getting Started

Idea #1: A few days before your group meets, get a few select food items—meat, eggs, and so on—and let them rot somewhere. Then take the stinky mess and put it in an old, plastic container with a tight lid. Bring it to the meeting with you.

At the meeting place, write the following passage on a whiteboard or via an overhead projector: FOR THE WAGES OF SIN IS DEATH, BUT THE GIFT OF GOD IS ETERNAL LIFE IN CHRIST JESUS OUR LORD.—ROMANS 6:23

Begin by saying something like this:

> Isn't it funny how we can read and hear a passage from the Bible our whole lives and not really get the point? For some people, this passage may be familiar—but judging by their actions and attitudes, they don't seem to get it at all. As we get thinking about our study, I'd like to add a dimension to this verse that you might receive if a "scratch 'n' sniff Bible" were ever invented. When God says the wages of sin is DEATH—this is probably what would fill your nostrils when you came upon this passage.

Pop the lid off your container of death and pass it around. Transition to the lesson by saying something like this:

> We're going to take a look at the subject of sin—and how we can avoid stinking like death to high heaven.

Put the lid back on the container (and take it out of the room before continuing).

Idea #2: Get a few regular mushrooms and slice them up. Put the contents into two small boxes. Label one box MUSHROOMS and label the other box TOADSTOOLS. (Go online and find the scientific name for a few other varieties and add them to your labels as well.) Bring the boxes to the meeting.

Tell your students you've brought them some healthy treats that you found growing near your yard. Pass the boxes around and invite kids to sample the goodies.

You may get some reactions to the toadstool box.

Play dumb. Say, "Gee, they looked like mushrooms, or I don't know, do you think they're poisonous? Why don't you try them and see?" Some of your kids will have great faith in you, some will be skeptics, and some will figure that if you can't tell the difference between a mushroom and a toadstool—then they're not about to taste anything.

Wrap up this little object lesson by nibbling a piece of "toadstool" and saying something like this:

> **The reason for your caution and concern about my little snack is that you don't want to poison yourselves—and that's a good thing! But interestingly, many of us who are so careful about what we put into our bodies will, without much inspection, take things into our souls that make them sin-sick. Let's consider that right now.**

Another variation of Idea #2 is to get a variety of mushrooms and toadstools (or even photos of them), number them—but don't name them or describe them in any way. Ask your students to play "Toadstool Roulette" by picking the one they would use for edible purposes. After the students have all chosen a sample, tell them which ones are safe to eat and which ones could kill them. Find out how many of your students would have been dead. Wrap up the same way.

Bible Study

Idea #1: Break into groups of four to five students each. Assign each group at least one of the following case studies (add or change as you desire):

- Achan (Joshua 7:1-26)
- The minister's rotten sons (1 Samuel 2:22-25, 29, 3:11-14)
- David and Bathsheba (2 Samuel 11:2-27, 12:1-23; Psalm 38:1-22)
- The Pharisees (Matthew 6:2-8, 16-18, 15:1-9, 23:2-33)
- The rich young ruler and Jesus (Mark 10:17-22)
- The rich man and Lazarus (Luke 16:19-31)
- The woman caught in adultery (John 8)
- Ananias and Sapphira (Acts 5:1-11)
- "One-up-on-you" church members (1 Corinthians 1:12-16)
- Perverted church members (1 Corinthians 5:1-5)
- Snotty church members (James 2:1-4)

Then have each group answer the following questions regarding their passage—

- Identify a kind of sin that rises to the surface in this passage.
- Report the kind of problems this sin led to or was likely to lead to.
- Give a modern example of this kind of sin.
- Tell the ending of the story—was it a positive ending, negative ending, or a mixed bag?

After your students have reported back, take a little time to discuss how most of these Bible figures—even with their sin and disobedience problems—either knew a lot about the Scriptures or claimed to be believers.

Idea #2: Track the life of the Prodigal Son (Luke 15:11-32) in a brief, modern retelling. (Jonathan McKee does a great job with this concept. He calls it "Everett's Story" and it's found on pages 123-132 of his book, *Do They Run When They See You Coming?* Youth Specialties/Zondervan, 2004.) You can also have students create their own versions of the Prodigal Son story (set in modern times) and let them share their tales with the group.

Wrap Up

Transition to *The Sin Vibe* video clip by saying something like this:

> **Here's a short video clip that offers a pretty good summary of the final paycheck sin delivers. Let's take a look at it.**

Show *The Sin Vibe* video clip.

Following the clip, briefly discuss the good news that sin has been defeated on the cross. Close by reading Romans 7:24-25 and then, in prayer, thank God for defeating the power of sin in our lives.

Talk to Me! Talksheet

Take a crack at answering these tough questions. See if you can support your opinions with the Bible.

- How would you define the word *sin*?
- Can sin be something you don't do? Explain.
- Are all sins equal? Explain your answer.
- Why do you think we do things that we clearly know are wrong?
- Why does sin often seem fun? What's deceptive about this?
- Are all people attracted to the same kinds of sins? Why or why not?
- Do people who couldn't care less about God know that they're sinners, too? Why or why not?
- What happens to us when we sin?
- What role does the Holy Spirit play when we sin?
- What does being caught in a nasty sin do to a person?
- Offer an example of sins that are against man and God and sins that are only against God.
- What happens to us when we refuse to admit our sins?
- Are there sins that don't harm anyone but the people committing them?

Permission granted to reproduce this talksheet only for use in buyer's own youth group. This page can be downloaded from the Web site for this book:

www.YouthSpecialties.com/store/downloads   code: highway 5
© YouthSpecialties. www.YouthSpecialties.com

The Sin Vibe

Production Notes: The Sin Vibe

Director: Javad Shadzi

Sins are like huge boogers in our noses. Let's face it: we all get boogers. We all pick boogers—we know it's gross, but we can't seem to ignore the fact that they're there. Sometimes we pick them in public, but usually it happens behind closed doors or when cruising down the freeway to the drone of the latest Top-40 song. Boogers just appear. We don't feel them forming, but all of a sudden we turn our heads just the right way and—sure enough—the pressure of a newly formed nugget makes its presence known to our nostrils.

Problem is, we need boogers. Without them, horrible toxins and infections couldn't be cleansed from our sinuses. Somehow, in the grand scheme of things, these salty little gremlins bring us closer to good health and sustenance.

Like I said, boogers are a lot like sin. Imagine if we weren't able to cleanse our souls of infection? What if there was no way to deal with sin? What would happen to us? I asked myself these questions while we pondered this piece of the curriculum, and the image of a beautiful flower dying—wilting from within—appeared to me.

Sin is real and—for every human who has ever lived—a reality. The point of sin (and life, for that matter) isn't that it's horrible, and it will surely defeat us; the point of sin is that it's the reality in which we live. As depressing and chaotic as that sounds, God has promised us renewed life over sin. (Are you hearing this?)

Life is tough a lot of the time. God knows this—it's no secret to him. But God is bigger than all the horrible sins he already knows we'll commit and struggle with.

That's the "good news"—God uses the most beautiful things on earth, and even the most horrible things on earth, to glorify himself and transform us in the process.

So the next time you feel that "nostril nugget" stuck to the inside of your nose, know that you'll always have boogers. They're gross, but they play their roles and serve a higher purpose—your greater health. Boogers aren't the point of your nose—being free from toxins is.

Sin isn't just the reality we live in, it's what we're redeemed from, despite how hopeless it may often seem.

More compelling Highway Visual Curriculum to help your students face tough subjects and draw closer to God.

Gimme God
The Journey of Your Unfolding Faith
Gimme God focuses on the wonderful journey from simply wanting God to needing him like oxygen.

RETAIL $24.99
ISBN 0310258308

Life Rollercoaster
Surviving the Twists, Turns, and Drops
Life Rollercoaster covers five topics important to teens: friends and peer pressure, parents and other adults, God, acceptance, and community.

RETAIL $24.99
ISBN 0310254221

Stuck in a Rut
Power, Sex, Food, and Other Little Addictions
Stuck in a Rut explores why students are turning to the false gods of addiction in order to satisfy their inner emptiness.

RETAIL $24.99
ISBN 0310254426

What Do You Want?
Understanding God's Will
What Do You Want? encourages your students to focus on the action of living in Christ.

RETAIL $24.99
ISBN 0310258332

visit www.youthspecialties.com/store
or your local Christian bookstore

Youth Specialties

There are more than 200 passages in the Bible about God's fury toward oppression.

So, what are you going to do about that?

Here's a good place to start. This video-based curriculum details the issues surrounding oppression and real solutions. These five sessions will motivate your students to help end injustice across the globe and across the street.

The Justice Mission
A Video-enhanced Curriculum Reflecting the Heart of God for the Oppressed of the World
Jim Hancock, International Justice Mission

RETAIL $37.99
ISBN 031024255X

visit www.youthspecialties.com/store
or your local Christian bookstore

Everything you need for a great talk

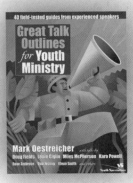

Great Talk Outlines for Youth Ministry
Mark Oestreicher
RETAIL $24.99
ISBN 0310238226

Great Talk Outlines for Youth Ministry 2
Mark Oestreicher
RETAIL $24.99
ISBN 0310252881

Ideal for youth pastors, volunteer youth workers, camp directors, or anyone who works with kids, the *Great Talk Outlines for Youth Ministry* books provide the tools to make talks less stressful and more successful. Each book contains 40 outlines from veteran youth workers that function as complete presentations or can be tailored for your group. Included is a CD-ROM of each outline in Microsoft Word® format.

visit **www.youthspecialties.com/store**
or your local Christian bookstore

Youth Specialties